Air Fryer Cookbook 2021

A Detailed Beginners Guide To Quick, Vibrant & Mouthwatering
Air Fryer Recipes For Living And Eating Well Every Day

CLARISSA HEWITT

Table of Contents

Breakfast Recipes

1. Milky Scrambled Eggs

Preparation Time: 10 minutes

Cooking time: 9 minutes

Servings: 2

Ingredients:

¾ cup milk

4 eggs

8 grape tomatoes, halved

½ cup Parmesan cheese, grated

1 tablespoon butter

Salt and black pepper, to taste

Directions:

Preheat the Air fryer to 360 o F and grease an Air fryer pan with butter.

Whisk together eggs with milk, salt and black pepper in a bowl.

Transfer the egg mixture into the prepared pan and place in the Air fryer.

Cook for about 6 minutes and stir in the grape tomatoes and cheese.

Cook for about 3 minutes and serve warm.

Nutrition:

Calories: 351, Fat: 22g, Carbohydrates: 25.2g, Sugar: 17.7g, Protein: 26.4g, Sodium: 422mg

2. Toasties and Sausage in Egg Pond

Preparation Time: 10 minutes

Cooking time: 22 minutes

Servings: 2

Ingredients:

3 eggs

2 cooked sausages, sliced

1 bread slice, cut into sticks

1/8 cup mozzarella cheese, grated

1/8 cup Parmesan cheese, grated

¼ cup cream

Directions:

Preheat the Air fryer to 365 o F and grease 2 ramekins lightly.

Whisk together eggs with cream in a bowl and place in the ramekins.

Stir in the bread and sausage slices in the egg mixture and top with cheese.

Transfer the ramekins in the Air fryer basket and cook for about 22 minutes.

Dish out and serve warm.

Nutrition:

Calories: 261, Fat: 18.8g, Carbohydrates: 4.2g, Sugar: 1.3g, Protein: 18.3g, Sodium: 428mg

3. Banana Bread

Preparation Time: 10 minutes

Cooking time: 20 minutes

Servings: 8

Ingredients:

1 1/3 cups flour

1 teaspoon baking soda

1 teaspoon baking powder

½ cup milk

3 bananas, peeled and sliced

2/3 cup sugar

1 teaspoon ground cinnamon

1 teaspoon salt

½ cup olive oil

Directions:

Preheat the Air fryer to 330 o F and grease a loaf pan.

Mix together all the dry ingredients with the wet ingredients to form a dough.

Place the dough into the prepared loaf pan and transfer into an air fryer basket.

Cook for about 20 minutes and remove from air fryer.

Cut the bread into desired size slices and serve warm.

Nutrition:

Calories: 295, Fat: 13.3g, Carbohydrates: 44g, Sugar: 22.8g, Protein: 3.1g, Sodium: 458mg

Lunch Recipes

4. Easiest Tuna Cobbler Ever

Preparation time: 15 min Cooking time: 25 min

Servings: 4

Ingredients:

Water, cold (1/3 cup)

Tuna, canned, drained (10 ounces)

Sweet pickle relish (2 tablespoons)

Mixed vegetables, frozen (1 ½ cups)

Soup, cream of chicken, condensed (10 ¾ ounces)

Pimientos, sliced, drained (2 ounces)

Lemon juice (1 teaspoon)

Paprika

Directions:

Preheat the air fryer at 375 degrees Fahrenheit.

Mist cooking spray into a round casserole (1 ½ quarts).

Mix the frozen vegetables with milk, soup, lemon juice, relish, pimientos, and tuna in a saucepan. Cook for six to eight minutes over medium heat.

Fill the casserole with the tuna mixture.

Mix the biscuit mix with cold water to form a soft dough. Beat for half a minute before dropping by four spoonfuls into the casserole.

Dust the dish with paprika before air-frying for twenty to twenty-five minutes.

Nutrition: Calories 320 Fat 11.0 g Protein 28.0 g Carbohydrates 31.0 g

5. Deliciously Homemade Pork Buns

Preparation time: 20 min

Cooking time: 25 min

Servings: 8

Ingredients:

Green onions, sliced thinly (3 pieces)

Egg, beaten (1 piece)

Pulled pork, diced, w/ barbecue sauce (1 cup)

Buttermilk biscuits, refrigerated (16 1/3 ounces)

Soy sauce (1 teaspoon)

Directions:

Preheat the air fryer at 325 degrees Fahrenheit.

Use parchment paper to line your baking sheet.

Combine pork with green onions.

Separate and press the dough to form 8 four-inch rounds.

Fill each biscuit round's center with two tablespoons of pork mixture. Cover with the dough edges and seal by pinching. Arrange the buns on the sheet and brush with a mixture of soy sauce and egg.

Cook in the air fryer for twenty to twenty-five minutes.

Nutrition: Calories 240 Fat 9.0 g Protein 8.0 g Carbohydrates 29.0 g

Poultry Recipes

6. Pickled Poultry

Preparation time: 10 minutes

Cooking time: 25 minutes

Servings: 4

Ingredients:

600g of poultry, without bones or skin

3 white onions, peeled and cut into thin slices

5 garlic cloves, peeled and sliced

3 dl olive oil

1 dl apple cider vinegar

½ l white wine

2 bay leaves

5 g peppercorns

Flour

Pepper

Salt

Directions:

Rub the bird in dice that we will pepper and flour

Put a pan with oil on the fire. When the oil is hot, fry the floured meat dice in it until golden brown. Take them out and reserve, placing them in a clay or oven dish. Strain the oil in which you have fried the meat

Preheat the oven to 170° C

Put the already cast oil in another pan over the fire. Sauté the garlic and onions in it. Add the white wine and let cook about 3 minutes. Remove the pan from the heat, add the vinegar to the oil and wine. Remove, rectify salt, and pour this mixture into the source where you had left the bird dice. Introduce the source in the oven, lower the temperature to 140°C and bake for 1 and ½ hours. Remove the source from the oven and let it stand at room temperature

When the source is cold, put it in the fridge and let it rest a few hours before serving.

Nutrition:

Calories: 232

Fat: 15g

Carbohydrates: 5.89g

Protein: 18.2g

Sugar: 1.72g

Cholesterol: 141mg

7. Cordon Bleu Chicken Breast

Preparation time: 10 minutes

Cooking time: 40 minutes

Servings: 6

Ingredients:

4 flattened chicken breasts

8 slices of ham

16 slices of Swiss cheese

2 tsp fresh thyme

¼ cup flour

1 cup of ground bread

2 tsp melted butter

2 eggs

1 clove garlic finely chopped

pam cooking spray

Directions:

Preheat the air fryer to 350 degrees Fahrenheit (180 °C), set timer to 5 minutes. Then, flatten chicken breasts.

Fill the chicken breasts with two slices of cheese, then 2 slices of ham and finally 2 slices of cheese and roll up. Use a stick if necessary, to save the shape.

Mix the ground bread with the thyme, the garlic finely chopped, with the melted butter and with salt and pepper.
Beat the eggs. Season the flour with salt and pepper.
Pass the chicken rolls first through the flour, then through the egg and finally through the breadcrumbs.
Bake until the breasts are cooked, about 20 minutes.
Alternatively, before putting the chicken breasts in the air fryer you can fry them in a little butter and then finish cooking in the air fryer for 13-15 minutes.

Nutrition:

Calories: 387

Fat: 20g

Carbohydrates: 18g

Protein: 33g

Sugar: 0g

Cholesterol: 42mg

8. Fried Chicken

Preparation time: 15 minutes

Cooking time: 25 minutes

Servings: 4

Ingredients:

1kg of chicken chopped into small pieces

Garlic powder

Salt

Ground pepper

1 little grated ginger

1 lemon

Extra virgin olive oil

Directions:

Put the chicken in a large bowl.

Add the lemon juice and pepper.

Add some grated ginger and mix well.

Leave 15 minutes in the refrigerator.

Add now a jet of extra virgin olive oil and mix.

Put the chicken in the air fryer, if it does not fit in a batch, it is put in two.

Select 180 degrees, 25 minutes.

Shake the baskets a few times so that the chicken rotates and is made on all sides.

If you want to pass the chicken for flour, before putting it in the basket and frying, you can do it.

Nutrition:

Calories: 4

Fat: 3.3g

Carbohydrates: 2.3g

Protein: 2.5g

Sugar: 0.1g

Cholesterol: 8.8mg

9. Rolls Stuffed with Broccoli and Carrots with Chicken

Preparation time: 15 minutes

Cooking time: 25 minutes

Servings: 4

Ingredients:

8 sheets of rice pasta

1 chicken breast

1 onion

1 carrot

150g broccolis

1 can of sweet corn

Extra virgin olive oil

Salt

Ground pepper

Soy sauce

1 bag of rice three delicacies

Directions:

Start with the vegetable that you have to cook previously, stop them, peel the carrot.

Cut the carrot and broccoli as small as you can. Add the broccolis and the carrot to a pot with boiling water and let cook a few minutes, they have to be tender, but not too much, that crunch a little.

Drain well and reserve.

Cut the onion into julienne.

Cut the breast into strips.

In the Wok, put some extra virgin olive oil.

Add to the wok when it is hot, the onion and the chicken breast.

Sauté well until the chicken is cooked.

Drain the corn and add to the wok along with the broccolis and the carrot.

Sauté so that the ingredients are mixed.

Add salt, ground pepper and a little soy sauce.

Mix well and let the filling cool.

Hydrate the rice pasta sheets.

Spread on the worktable and distribute the filling between the sheets of rice paste.

Assemble the rolls and paint with a little oil.

Put in the air fryer, those who enter do not pile up.

Select 10 minutes 200 degrees.

When you have all the rolls made, the first ones will have cooled, because to solve it, you now place all the rolls already cooked inside the air fryer, now it does not matter that they are piled up.

Select 180 degrees, 5 minutes.

Make while the rice as indicated by the manufacturer in its bag.

Serve the rice with the rolls.

Nutrition:

Calories: 125

Fat: 4.58g

Carbohydrates: 16.83g

Protein: 4.69g

Sugar: 4.43g

Cholesterol: 0mg

Fish and Seafood Recipes

10. Tuna Pie

Preparation time: 10 minutes

Cooking time: 30 minutes

Servings: 4

Ingredients:

2 hard-boiled eggs

2 tuna cans

200 ml fried tomato

1 sheet of broken dough.

Directions:

Cut the eggs into small pieces and mix with the tuna and tomato.

Spread the sheet of broken dough and cut into two equal squares.

Put the mixture of tuna, eggs, and tomato on one of the squares.

Cover with the other, join at the ends and decorate with leftover little pieces.

Preheat the air fryer a few minutes at 1800C.

Enter in the air fryer basket and set the timer for 15 minutes at 1800C

Nutrition:

Calories: 244

Fat: 13.67g

Carbohydrates: 21.06g

Protein: 8.72g

Sugar: 0.22g

Cholesterol: 59mg

11. Tuna Puff Pastry

Preparation time: 5 minutes

Cooking time: 15 minutes

Servings: 2

Ingredients:

2 square puff pastry dough, bought ready

1 egg (white and yolk separated)

½ cup tuna tea

½ cup chopped parsley tea

½ cup chopped tea olives

Salt and pepper to taste

Directions:

Preheat the air fryer. Set the timer of 5 minutes and the temperature to 200C.

Mix the tuna with olives and parsley. Season to taste and set aside. Place half of the filling in each dough and fold in half. Brush with egg white and close gently. After closing, make two small cuts at the top of the air outlet. Brush with the egg yolk.

Place in the basket of the air fryer. Set the time to 10 minutes and press the power button.

Nutrition:

Calories: 291

Fat: 16g

Carbohydrates: 26g

Protein: 8g

Sugar: 0g

Cholesterol: 0

Meat Recipes

12. Smoked Beef Mix

Preparation time: 5 minutes

Cooking time: 20 minutes

Servings: 4

Ingredients

1pound beef stew meat, roughly cubed

1tablespoon smoked paprika

½ cup beef stock

½ teaspoon garam masala

2tablespoons olive oil

A pinch of salt and black pepper

Directions

In the air fryer's basket, mix the beef with the smoked paprika and the other ingredients, toss and cook at 390 degrees F for 20 minutes on each side.

Divide between plates and serve.

Nutrition: Calories 274, Fat 12, Fiber 4, Carbs 6, Protein 17

13. Marjoram Pork Mix

Preparation time: 5 minutes

Cooking time: 25 minutes

Servings: 4

INGREDIENTS

2pounds pork stew meat, roughly cubed

1tablespoon marjoram, chopped

1cup heavy cream

2tablespoons olive oil

Salt and black pepper to the taste

2garlic cloves, minced

Directions

Heat up a pan that fits the air fryer with the oil over medium-high heat, add the meat and brown for 5 minutes

Add the rest of the ingredients, toss, put the pan in the fryer and cook at 400 degrees F for 20 minutes more.

Divide between plates and serve.

Nutrition: Calories 274, Fat 14, Fiber 3, Carbs 6, Protein 14

14. Nutmeg Lamb

Preparation time: 5 minutes

Cooking time: 30 minutes

Servings: 4

Ingredients

1pound lamb stew meat, cubed

2teaspoons nutmeg, ground

1teaspoon coriander, ground

1cup heavy cream

2tablespoons olive oil

2tablespoons chives, chopped

Salt and black pepper to the taste

DIRECTIONS

In the air fryer's pan, mix the lamb with the nutmeg and the other ingredients, put the pan in the air fryer and cook at 380 degrees F for 30 minutes.

Divide everything into bowls and serve.

Nutrition: Calories 287, Fat 13, Fiber 2, Carbs 6, Protein 12

Side Dish Recipes

15. Simple Squash Casserole

Preparation time: 20 min

Cooking time: 40 min

Servings: 6

Ingredients:

Yellow summer squash, medium, sliced thinly (1 piece)

Thyme leaves, fresh, chopped (1 tablespoon)

Salt (1/2 teaspoon)

Italian cheese blend, gluten free, shredded (1/2 cup)

Olive oil, extra virgin (1 tablespoon)

Zucchini, medium, sliced thinly (1 piece)

Onion, diced (1/2 cup)

Brown rice, cooked (1 cup)

Plum tomato, diced (1 piece)

Pepper (1/8 teaspoon)

Directions:

Preheat air fryer to 375 degrees Fahrenheit.

Mist cooking spray onto a gratin dish.

Combine rice, onion, tomato, pepper, salt (1/4 teaspoon), oil, and ½ thyme leaves. Spread evenly into gratin dish and layer on top with squash and zucchini. Sprinkle with remaining salt (1/4 teaspoon) and thyme.

Cover and air-fry for twenty minutes. Top with cheese and air-fry for another ten to twelve minutes.

Nutrition: Calories 110 Fat 5.0 g Protein 4.0 g Carbohydrates 12.0 g

16. Delicious Ginger Pork Lasagna

Preparation time: 45 min

Cooking time: 45 min

Servings: 8

Ingredients:

Thai basil leaves, fresh, sliced thinly (2 tablespoons)

Butter (1 tablespoon)

Garlic cloves, minced (2 pieces)

Ricotta cheese, part skim (15 ounces)

Wonton wrappers, square (48 pieces)

Green onion greens & whites, separated, sliced thinly (4 pieces)

Fish sauce (1 tablespoon)

Parmesan cheese, shredded (1 tablespoon)

Sesame oil, toasted (1 tablespoon)

Ground pork (1 pound)

Gingerroot, fresh, minced (1 tablespoon)

Tomato sauce (15 ounces)

Chili garlic sauce (1 tablespoon)

Coconut milk (1/2 cup)

Directions:

Preheat air fryer at 325 degrees Fahrenheit.

Mist cooking spray onto a baking dish.

In skillet heated on medium, cook pork in butter and sesame oil for eight to ten minutes. Stir in garlic, green onion whites, and gingerroot and cook for one to two minutes. Stir in fish sauce, chili garlic sauce, and tomato sauce. Cook on gentle simmer.

Combine coconut milk, ricotta cheese, and parmesan cheese (1 cup).

Arrange 8 overlapping wonton wrappers in baking dish to line bottom, then top with a second layer of eight wrappers. Spread on top 1/3 of cheese mixture, and layer with 1/3 of pork mixture. Repeat layering twice and finish by topping with parmesan cheese.

Cover dish with foil and air-fry for thirty minutes. Remove foil and air-fry for another ten to fifteen minutes.

Serve topped with basil and green onion greens.

Nutrition: Calories 480 Fat 24.0 g Protein 28.0 g Carbohydrates 37.0 g

Dessert Recipes

17. Carrot brownies

Preparation time: 10 minutes

Cooking time: 25 minutes

Servings: 8

Ingredients:

1 teaspoon almond extract

2 eggs, whisked

½ cup butter, melted

4 tablespoons sugar

2 cups almond flour

½ cup carrot, peeled and grated

Directions:

In a bowl, combine the eggs with the butter and the other ingredients, whisk, spread this into a pan that fits your air fryer, introduce in the fryer and cook at 340 degrees f for 25 minutes.

Cool down, slice and serve.

Nutrition: calories 230, fat 12, fiber 2, carbs 12, protein 5

18. Yogurt cake

Preparation time: 10 minutes

Cooking time: 30 minutes

Servings: 8

Ingredients:

6 eggs, whisked

1 teaspoon vanilla extract

1 teaspoon baking soda

9 ounces almond flour

4 tablespoons sugar

2 cups yogurt

Directions:

In a blender, combine the eggs with the vanilla and the other ingredients, pulse, spread into a cake pan lined with parchment paper, put it in the air fryer and cook at 330 degrees f for 30 minutes.

Cool the cake down, slice and serve.

Nutrition: calories 231, fat 13, fiber 2, carbs 11, protein 5

19. Chocolate ramekins

Preparation time: 10 minutes

Cooking time: 20 minutes

Servings: 4

Ingredients:

2 cups cream cheese, soft

3 tablespoons sugar

4 eggs, whisked

1 teaspoon vanilla extract

½ cup heavy cream

2 cups white chocolate, melted

Directions:

In a bowl combine the cream cheese with the sugar and the other ingredients, whisk well, divide into 4 ramekins, put them in the air fryer's basket and cook at 370 degrees f for 20 minutes.

Serve cold.

Nutrition: calories 261, fat 12, fiber 6, carbs 12, protein 6

20. Grapes cake

Preparation time: 10 minutes

Cooking time: 25 minutes

Servings: 8

Ingredients:

1 cup coconut flour

1 teaspoon baking powder

¾ teaspoon almond extract

¾ cup sugar

Cooking spray

1 cup heavy cream

2 cup grapes, halved

1 egg, whisked

Directions:

In a bowl, combine the flour with the baking powder and the other ingredients except the cooking spray and whisk well.

Grease a cake pan with cooking spray, pour the cake batter inside, spread, introduce the pan in the air fryer and cook at 330 degrees f for 25 minutes.

Cool the cake down, slice and serve.

Nutrition: calories 214, fat 9, fiber 3, carbs 14, protein 8

Vegetarian Recipes

21. Garlic Tomatoes

Preparation Time: 5 minutes

Cooking Time: 15 minutes

Servings: 4

Ingredients:

1 lb. cherry tomatoes; halved

6 garlic cloves; minced

1 tbsp. olive oil

1 tbsp. dill; chopped.

1 tbsp. balsamic vinegar

Salt and black pepper to taste.

Directions:

In a pan that fits the air fryer, combine all the ingredients, toss gently.

Put the pan in the air fryer and cook at 380°F for 15 minutes

Divide between plates and serve.

Nutrition: Calories: 121; Fat: 3g; Fiber: 2g; Carbs: 4g; Protein: 6g

22. Zucchini and Olives

Preparation Time: 5 minutes

Cooking Time: 12 minutes

Servings: 4

Ingredients:

4 zucchinis; sliced

2 tbsp. olive oil

1 cup kalamata olives, pitted

2 tbsp. lime juice

2 tsp. balsamic vinegar

Salt and black pepper to taste.

Directions:

In a pan that fits your air fryer, mix the olives with all the other ingredients, toss, introduce in the fryer and cook at 390°F for 12 minutes

Divide the mix between plates and serve.

Nutrition: Calories: 150; Fat: 4g; Fiber: 2g; Carbs: 4g; Protein: 5g

23. Bacon Asparagus

Preparation Time: 5 minutes

Cooking Time: 10 minutes

Servings: 4

Ingredients:

2 lb. asparagus, trimmed

4 bacon slices, cooked and crumbled

1 cup cheddar cheese, shredded

4 garlic cloves; minced

2 tbsp. olive oil

Directions:

Take a bowl and mix the asparagus with the other ingredients except the bacon, toss and put in your air fryer's basket

Cook at 400°F for 10 minutes, divide between plates, sprinkle the bacon on top and serve.

Nutrition: Calories: 172; Fat: 6g; Fiber: 2g; Carbs: 5g; Protein: 8g

Brunch Recipes

24. Omelette Frittata

Preparation Time: 10 minutes

Cooking Time: 6 minutes

Servings: 2

Ingredients:

3 eggs, lightly beaten

2 tbsp cheddar cheese, shredded

2 tbsp heavy cream

2 mushrooms, sliced

1/4 small onion, chopped

1/4 bell pepper, diced

Pepper

Salt

Directions:

In a bowl, whisk eggs with cream, vegetables, pepper, and salt.

Preheat the air fryer to 400 F.

Pour egg mixture into the air fryer pan. Place pan in air fryer basket and cook for 5 minutes.

Add shredded cheese on top of the frittata and cook for 1 minute more.

Serve and enjoy.

Nutrition:

Calories 160

Fat 10 g

Carbohydrates 4 g

Sugar 2 g

Protein 12 g

Cholesterol 255 mg

25. Cheese Soufflés

Preparation Time: 10 minutes

Cooking Time: 6 minutes

Servings: 8

Ingredients:

6 large eggs, separated

3/4 cup heavy cream

1/4 tsp cayenne pepper

1/2 tsp xanthan gum

1/2 tsp pepper

1/4 tsp cream of tartar

2 tbsp chives, chopped

2 cups cheddar cheese, shredded

1 tsp salt

Directions:

Preheat the air fryer to 325 F.

Spray eight ramekins with cooking spray. Set aside.

In a bowl, whisk together almond flour, cayenne pepper, pepper, salt, and xanthan gum.

Slowly add heavy cream and mix to combine.

Whisk in egg yolks, chives, and cheese until well combined.

In a large bowl, add egg whites and cream of tartar and beat until stiff peaks form.

Fold egg white mixture into the almond flour mixture until combined.

Pour mixture into the prepared ramekins. Divide ramekins in batches.

Place the first batch of ramekins into the air fryer basket.

Cook soufflé for 20 minutes.

Serve and enjoy.

Nutrition:

Calories 210

Fat 16 g

Carbohydrates 1 g

Sugar 0.5 g

Protein 12 g

Cholesterol 185 mg

26. Simple Egg Soufflé

Preparation Time: 5 minutes

Cooking Time: 8 minutes

Servings: 2

Ingredients:

2 eggs

1/4 tsp chili pepper

2 tbsp heavy cream

1/4 tsp pepper

1 tbsp parsley, chopped

Salt

Directions:

In a bowl, whisk eggs with remaining gradients.

Spray two ramekins with cooking spray.

Pour egg mixture into the prepared ramekins and place into the air fryer basket.

Cook soufflé at 390 F for 8 minutes.

Serve and enjoy.

Nutrition:

Calories 116

Fat 10 g

Carbohydrates 1.1 g

Sugar 0.4 g

Protein 6 g

Cholesterol 184 mg

27. Vegetable Egg Soufflé

Preparation Time: 10 minutes

Cooking Time: 20 minutes

Servings: 4

Ingredients:

4 large eggs

1 tsp onion powder

1 tsp garlic powder

1 tsp red pepper, crushed

1/2 cup broccoli florets, chopped

1/2 cup mushrooms, chopped

Directions:

Spray four ramekins with cooking spray and set aside.

In a bowl, whisk eggs with onion powder, garlic powder, and red pepper.

Add mushrooms and broccoli and stir well.

Pour egg mixture into the prepared ramekins and place ramekins into the air fryer basket.

Cook at 350 F for 15 minutes. Make sure souffle is cooked if souffle is not cooked then cook for 5 minutes more.

Serve and enjoy.

Nutrition:

Calories 91

Fat 5.1 g

Carbohydrates 4.7 g

Sugar 2.6 g

Protein 7.4 g

Cholesterol 186 mg

28. Asparagus Frittata

Preparation Time: 10 minutes

Cooking Time: 10 minutes

Servings: 4

Ingredients:

6 eggs

3 mushrooms, sliced

10 asparagus, chopped

1/4 cup half and half

2 tsp butter, melted

1 cup mozzarella cheese, shredded

1 tsp pepper

1 tsp salt

Directions:

Toss mushrooms and asparagus with melted butter and add into the air fryer basket.

Cook mushrooms and asparagus at 350 F for 5 minutes. Shake basket twice.

Meanwhile, in a bowl, whisk together eggs, half and half, pepper, and salt.

Transfer cook mushrooms and asparagus into the air fryer baking dish.

Pour egg mixture over mushrooms and asparagus.

Place dish in the air fryer and cook at 350 F for 5 minutes or until eggs are set.

Slice and serve.

Nutrition:

Calories 211

Fat 13 g

Carbohydrates 4 g

Sugar 1 g

Protein 16 g

Cholesterol 272 mg

29. Beer Coated Duck Breast

Preparation Time: 15 minutes

Cooking Time: 20 minutes

Servings: 2 servings

Ingredients

1 tablespoon olive oil

1 teaspoon mustard

1 tablespoon fresh thyme, chopped

1 cup beer

Salt and ground black pepper, as required

1 (10½-ounces) duck breast

6 cherry tomatoes

1 tablespoon balsamic vinegar

Directions

In a bowl, mix together the oil, mustard, thyme, beer, salt, and black pepper.

Add the duck breast and generously coat with marinade.

Cover and refrigerate for about 4 hours.

Set the temperature of Air Fryer to 390 degrees F.

With a piece of foil, cover the duck breast and arrange into an Air Fryer basket.

Air Fry for about 15 minutes.

Remove the foil from breast.

Now, set the temperature of Air Fryer to 355 degrees F. Grease the Air Fryer basket.

Place duck breast and tomatoes into the prepared Air Fryer basket.

Air Fry for about 5 minutes.

Remove from Air Fryer and place the duck breast onto a cutting board for about 5 minutes before slicing.

With a sharp knife, cut the duck breast into desired size slices and transfer onto serving plates.

Drizzle with vinegar and serve alongside the cherry tomatoes.

Nutrition

Calories: 332

Carbohydrate: 9.2g

Protein: 34.6g

Fat: 13.7g

Sugar: 2.5g

Sodium: 88mg

30. Duck Breast with Figs

Prep Time: 20 minutes

Cooking Time: 45 minutes

Servings: 2

Ingredients

2 cups fresh pomegranate juice

2 tablespoons lemon juice

3 tablespoons brown sugar

1 pound boneless duck breast

6 fresh figs, halved

1 teaspoon olive oil

Salt and ground black pepper, as required

1 tablespoon fresh thyme, chopped

Directions

In a medium saucepan, add the pomegranate juice, lemon juice, and brown sugar over medium heat and bring to a boil.

Now, lower the heat to low and cook for about 25 minutes until the mixture becomes thick.

Remove the pan from heat and let it cool slightly.

Set the temperature of Air Fryer to 400 degrees F. Grease an Air Fryer basket.

Score the fat of duck breasts several times using a sharp knife.

Sprinkle the duck breast with salt and black pepper.

Arrange duck breast into the prepared Air Fryer basket, skin side up.

Air Fry for about 14 minutes, flipping once halfway through.

Remove from Air Fryer and place the duck breast onto a cutting board for about 5-10 minutes.

Meanwhile, in a bowl, add the figs, oil, salt, and black pepper and toss to coat well.

Once again, set the temperature of Air Fryer to 400 degrees F. Grease the Air Fryer basket.

Arrange figs into the prepared basket in a single layer.

Air Fry for about 5 minutes.

Using a sharp knife, cut the duck breast into desired size slices and transfer onto serving plates alongside the roasted figs.

Drizzle with warm pomegranate juice mixture and serve with the garnishing of fresh thyme.

Nutrition:

Calories: 669

Carbohydrate: 90g

Protein: 519g

Fat: 12.1g

Sugar: 74g

Sodium: 110mg

Air fryer Bonus Recipes

1. Buffalo Cauliflower Bites

Ingredients:

- 1 cup of all-purpose flour
- One teaspoon of kosher salt
- One teaspoon of garlic powder
- One teaspoon of onion powder
- Two eggs
- 1/2 cup of whole milk
- 2 cups Panko breadcrumbs
- One large head of cauliflower, sliced into florets
- 1 1/2 cup of ranch dressing
- 1 cup of hot sauce
- Chopped parsley, for garnishing

Instructions:

1. In a small dish, mix the flour, salt, garlic powder, and onion. In a second cup, whisk the egg and milk together. Place the Breadcrumbs in a separate bowl.
2. Dip one flower of cauliflower into the flour mixture, then apply the mixture of eggs and then the

breadcrumbs. Repeat before you bread all of the cauliflower.

3. Without overcrowding, add some of the cauliflower to the fry basket. Pick the Fry configuration (8 minutes to 400F degrees).

4. Halfway swirl the tub. When time is up, cut the cauliflower with caution. Cook another 2-3 minutes if the larger parts aren't fork-tender. Repeat until the entire cauliflower is baked.

5. Meanwhile, whisk together the ranch and hot sauce in a large saucepan. Heat to dry, over low altitude. Put the cauliflower into the warm sauce and eat right away. Garnish with peregrinate.

2. Cheddar Scallion Biscuits

Ingredients

- 2 cups of all-purpose flour
- Two tablespoons of baking powder
- 1/2 teaspoon salt
- 1/2 cup (4 ounces or eight tablespoons) cold unsalted butter, sliced into eight parts
- 1 cup shredded cheddar cheese
- 1/4 cup crumbled bacon
- One scallion, minced
- 1 cup cold strong whipping cream

Instructions

1. Add the baking powder, flour, and salt in a bowl, using a pastry knife to remove the butter or use the fingers until the paste is crumbly and looks like little pebbles.
2. Add the cheese, ham, scallion, and cream and stir until it is moistened and a dough forms.
3. Knead the dough gently on a finely floured surface, about 3-4 times. Roll the dough to a thickness of ¾.

4. Cut about nine biscuits (you would need to pick the scraps and roll them out again) using a two 1/2-inch diameter cookie cutter.

5. Without overcrowding, add some of the biscuits to the fry bowl. Choose the environment for the bake, increase the temperature to 350 degrees F, and change the time to 20 minutes or to a golden brown. Take off the biscuits gently until the time is over. Repeat until the biscuits are all baked.

This chapter will present some more palatable air fryer recipes that can be served as appetizers.

3. Cheesy Garlic & Herb Pull-Apart Bread

Ingredients

- 1 round loaf of sourdough bread
- Three cloves of garlic, minced
- Two tablespoons of finely chopped parsley
- Eight tablespoons of butter melted
- 1 cup of shredded cheese mix (cheddar, Monty jack, mozzarella, etc.)

Instructions

1. Split the bread into 1-inch slices; be careful not to split it all the way to the loaf's middle. Rotate, and repeat, 90 degrees.
2. Remove the sliced bread pieces and put them softly together with the shredded cheese.
3. Blend the garlic, parsley, and butter together in a little cup, then rub over the crust.
4. Place the fry configuration in your air fryer basket at 400 degrees F, minimize the time to ten minutes and bake until the cheese is melted and the surface is crispy and crisp.

4. Sweet Potato Fries with Sriracha Mayonnaise

<u>Ingredients</u>

- One big sweet potato, sliced and cut into 1/4-inch long strips
- 1/4 cup cornstarch
- One teaspoon kosher salt
- One teaspoon garlic powder
- 1/2 teaspoon paprika
- Two tablespoons of olive oil
- 1/2 cup mayonnaise
- Two tablespoons sriracha
- Two teaspoons of lemon juice
- Chopped parsley, for garnish

<u>Instructions</u>

1. Apply the sweet potato strips to a broad zip-top plastic container. Fill the bag with the cornstarch, oil, garlic powder, and paprika.
2. Shake to paint the potatoes full.
3. Pour the oil into the bag and shake to paint.
4. Without overcrowding, add some of the fries to the fry tub.

5. Use the Fry setting (400F degrees) and change the time to 15 minutes or until the inside is tendered, and the outside is crispy.

6. To hit your ideal crispness, add an additional 5 minutes if needed. Halfway shake the tub. When time is up, cut the fries carefully. Repeat until they prepare all the fries.

7. Whisk the mayonnaise, sriracha, and lemon juice combined, when doing so.

8. Serve the fries with mayonnaise sriracha and chopped parsley immediately.

5.   Mozzarella Cheese Balls

Ingredients

- 8 ounces mozzarella ciliegine (cherry-sized mozzarella balls), washed and patted dry
- 1/4 cup all-purpose flour
- 1/4 tablespoon kosher salt
- One egg
- 1/2 cup Panko breadcrumbs
- 1/4 cup grated Parmesan cheese
- Chopped parsley and marinara sauce, for serving

Instructions

1. In a dish, mix the flour and salt. Beat the egg gently in a second, shallow cup. Combine the breadcrumbs and cheese into a single, small dish.
2. Operating for one ball at a time, dredge in a mixture of flour, then milk, and breadcrumbs.
3. Place on a tray in a single plate. Freeze for 2 hours max.
4. Avoid overcrowding add a few balls to the fry bowl. Use the Setup Fry (400F degrees) and set the time to 6 minutes.

5. When time is up, apply with caution. Repeat until the balls are all fried.

6. Serve with parsley and marinara sauce right away.

6. Loaded Baked Potatoes

Ingredients

- 4 Small russet potatoes

- 1/2 cup sliced Mexican blend cheese

- Three strips of grilled bacon, diced

- Sour cream

- One teaspoon of minced chives

Instructions

1. Scrub the potatoes and poke the tines of a fork all over.

2. Place your air fryer in the basket and click the fry level to 400 degrees after Scaling up the time to 40 minutes.

3. Cook the potatoes until tender, with more or less time depending on the size you may require.

4. Cut, let sit at room temperature for about 5 minutes, then slice down the middle in half and scatter two teaspoons of cheese on top.

5. Place it back again in the air fryer for 1-2 minutes to melt.

6. Cut and finish with a dollop of sour cream, bacon diced, and chives sliced.

7.

7. Parmesan Zucchini Fries with Herb Dipping Sauce

Ingredients

- 2 Medium zucchini
- 1 cup panko
- 1 cup of Italian style bread crumbs
- 1 cup of finely ground parmesan cheese
- One egg + 2 tablespoons of water Salt and black pepper

For the dressing:

3/4 cup of Greek yogurt 1/4 cup of sour cream one tablespoon of hazelnut parsley one tablespoon of hazelnut chives one lemon juiced salt and pigment to fit

Instructions

1. Cut the zucchini in half lengthwise and after that into sticks no more than half-inch thick and four inches long.
2. Whisk the water and egg in a bowl and season with salt and pepper.
3. Mix the panko, bread crumbs, parmesan cheese & salt, and pepper in a shallow bowl.

85

4. Working in small amounts, dip the zucchini into the milk, then cover them in the breadcrumbs.

5. Put in the air fryer basket in a plate, click the fry setting at 400 degrees F, and reduce the cooking time to 10 minutes. Shake the bowl in half for better preparation. After 10 minutes, test and add 1-2 minutes of extra cooking time if needed.

6. Remove gently, then season with kosher salt.

7. Repeat with remaining fried zucchini. When fried, chuck all the fries back into the air fryer to reheat for 2-3 minutes.

8. When the fries are heating up, mix the sauce together in a little cup, whisking sour cream, Greek yogurt, dill, parsley, chives, lemon juice, and salt and pepper together to compare.

8. Smoked Paprika and Parm Potato Wedges

<u>**Ingredients**</u>

- Two Yukon gold potatoes, sliced in 6 wedges each
- One tablespoon of olive oil (optional)
- 1/2 teaspoon of smoked paprika
- 1/4 teaspoon salt
- 1/4 cup of grated parmesan cheese

<u>**Instructions**</u>

1. Drain the potatoes and sliced into six wedges each. Put the wedges in a bowl and then drizzle with olive oil if necessary. Sprinkle over with salt and paprika.

2. Place the wedges in the basket of the air fryer and click the fry level to 400 degrees F. Shorten time to 20 minutes. After 10 minutes, the basket shake. Sprinkle the parmesan cheese thinly over the potatoes when the potatoes are tender, then cook for 2 minutes to brown the cheese

9. Roasted Chickpea Snacks

Ingredients

- Chickpeas 15-ounce
- One teaspoon olive oil
- 1/2 teaspoon lime juice
- Pinch cayenne pepper
- Pinch cumin

Instructions

1. Wash and rinse chickpeas and pat dry. Place them in a little bowl and apply the oil and lime juice to drizzle. Remove the salt, pepper, cumin, and mix to shake.

2. Add the chickpeas in the air fryer basket. At 400 degrees F, click the fry setting and raising the time to 15 minutes.

3. During cooking, shake the basket several times to ensure cooking is correct.

4. Around 15 minutes, check a chickpea to see if it's done-it's going to be fully dried and crisp with no moisture in the middle. Continue to cook as desired, until the chickpeas are dry and crunchy. Let them cool fully before being placed in a sealed container.

10. "Marinated" Artichoke Hearts

If one like jarred marinated artichokes and don't like all of the oil they are swimming in, you will love these. They're good warm or chilled.

Ingredients

- One tablespoon of lemon juice
- One tablespoon of olive oil
- One teaspoon of oregano
- 1/2 teaspoon of thyme
- Pinch of red pepper flakes
- Pinch of garlic powder
- Pepper to taste
- Some black pepper grinds
- 12 ounces of frozen artichoke heart

Instructions

1. Layer the lemon juice, olive oil, oregano, thyme, garlic powder, salt, and pepper in a small cup. Attach the artichokes, and throw the artichokes to paint.

2. Place the artichokes in the basket of the air fryer and set the temperature manually to 350 degrees F. Set the timer 5 minutes.

3. Serve dry or cool until chilled.

CPSIA information can be obtained
at www.ICGtesting.com
Printed in the USA
BVHW091451220621
610211BV00003B/404